P9-AOZ-096

Not Yet, Yvette

Helen Ketteman

Illustrated by Irene Trivas

HARCOURT BRACE & COMPANY

Orlando Atlanta Austin Boston San Francisco Chicago Dallas New York
Toronto London

This edition is published by special arrangement with Albert Whitman
& Company.

Grateful acknowledgment is made to Albert Whitman & Company for
permission to reprint *Not Yet, Yvette* by Helen Ketteman, illustrated by Irene
Trivas. Text © 1992 by Helen Ketteman; illustrations © 1992 by Irene Trivas.

Printed in the United States of America

ISBN 0-15-302105-5

4 5 6 7 8 9 10   035   97 96 95

For my sisters,
Crissy, Mary Ann, and Jackie. H.K.

For Peter and Becca. I.T.

As soon as the door closed, Yvette asked, "Is it time yet, Dad?"

"Not yet, Yvette," he said. "We've got lots to do first."

Dad vacuumed and Yvette dusted. Before long, the whole house was clean.

"Is it time yet, Dad?"

"Not yet, Yvette. There's more to do."

In the kitchen, Dad found flour and sugar and other ingredients. Yvette got measuring spoons and a big bowl and a pan. They mixed and stirred and tasted and baked. The house smelled good.

Yvette watched through the oven door. "Is the cake ready yet, Dad?"

"Not yet, Yvette. It needs to bake a little more."
While it was cooking, Dad and Yvette cleaned up their mess.
"Now I think it's ready, Dad."
"You're right, Yvette!" he said. He set the cake on the counter to cool.

"We need to go out now," said Dad. They buttoned their coats.
It was rainy and cold, but today Yvette didn't mind.

At the store, Yvette helped Dad choose a present. "How about this red sweater?" he asked.

"Blue and white stripes are better," said Yvette.

Yvette looked and looked for something special.
"Cat earrings for a cat doctor!" said Yvette.
"You're a good shopper, Yvette," said Dad.
"Are we done shopping?"
"Not yet, Yvette."

Yvette found wrapping paper with cats on it.
"Terrific!" said Dad. "Now for paper plates and napkins."
"Let's get blue and white, to match the sweater," said Yvette.
"NOW is it time, Dad?"
"Not yet, Yvette. There's still more to do."

On a street corner, a lady was selling flowers at a stand. Yvette pulled on Dad's sleeve.

"Great idea, Yvette. You know how to plan a party!" Yvette chose a bouquet of daffodils and one of tulips.

When they got home, they arranged the flowers in a large vase and placed it on the dining room table. Yvette put three plates on the table, and Dad set the napkins and forks around.

Next, they got out vanilla, measuring
spoons, a big bowl, and other things.

"Where's the cocoa?" Dad asked.

Yvette got it for him. Soon, the chocolate
frosting was just right. Yvette helped
spread it on the cake. It looked beautiful.

Yvette and Dad licked the bowl. The
frosting tasted beautiful, too.

"Let's decorate the cake," said Yvette.
Dad handed her a tube of colored icing, and
Yvette drew a picture of a cat doctor and a cat.

"She'll like that, all right," said Dad.
"I'll help you write 'Happy Birthday.'"

"Is it time, yet?" Yvette asked.

"Not yet, Yvette. There's a little more to do. Where are the scissors?"

They went into the den, and Yvette got the scissors from a desk drawer. They cut the paper and wrapped their presents. Then they put the presents on the dining room table.

"We need something else," said Dad. He snapped his fingers. "I just remembered! Follow me, Yvette."

In the garage, Dad took a dusty box off a shelf. Yvette looked inside. "Decorations from our Fourth of July party last summer!" she said.

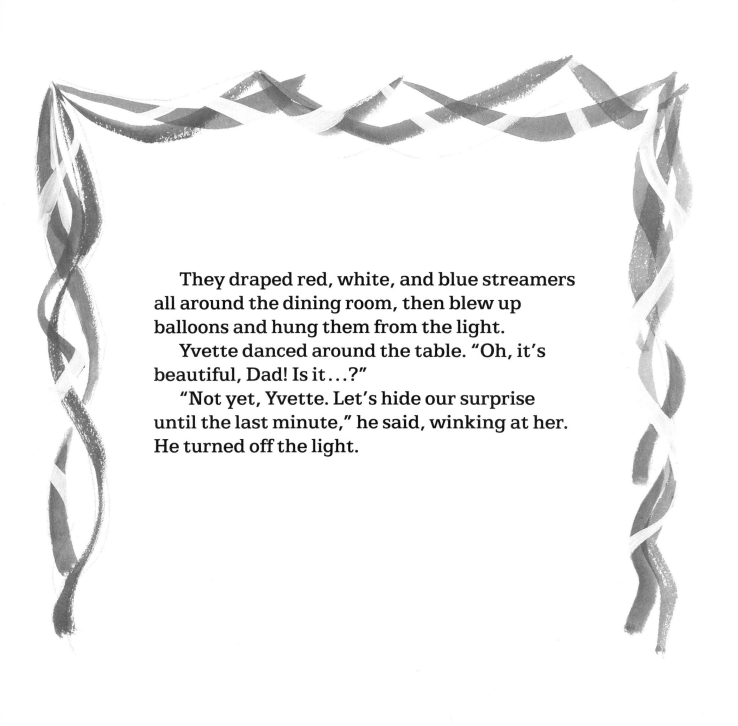

They draped red, white, and blue streamers
all around the dining room, then blew up
balloons and hung them from the light.

Yvette danced around the table. "Oh, it's
beautiful, Dad! Is it...?"

"Not yet, Yvette. Let's hide our surprise
until the last minute," he said, winking at her.
He turned off the light.

In the kitchen, they put candles on the cake. "Now," Dad said, looking at the clock, "it's almost time. I'll get ready to light the candles when you give me the word. You be the lookout."

Yvette sat by the front window, watching and waiting. It seemed like a long, long time before she saw the car coming down the street.

"She's coming!" Yvette cried. "Quick, Dad!"
"I'm lighting the candles!" he called. The front door opened.

"Is it time yet, Yvette?" Dad whispered.
"Yes, Dad—it's time!"

"Surprise, Mom!" they yelled. "Happy birthday!"